THE RAIN THAT DIDN'T FALL

NAUNIDH SACHDEVA

BlueRose ONE.com
Stories Matter
NewDelhi • London

BLUEROSE PUBLISHERS
India | U.K.

For permissions requests or inquiries regarding this publication, please contact:

BLUEROSE PUBLISHERS
www.BlueRoseONE.com
info@bluerosepublishers.com
+91 8882 898 898
+4407342408967

ISBN: 978-93-7139-989-0

Cover design: Daksh

First Edition: September 2025

PROLOGUE

Greetings readers, I am Naunidh Sachdeva, a 17-year-old who has had these poems written for quite a while but finally has them ready for the world to relish. They say when life throws something your way, you find either an escape or a coping mechanism. In the 17 years of my lifetime, I have had a fair share of adversities that life has thrown my way, and I think it will be completely valid to say that every time I came back stronger and more resilient but life is not a piece of cake, it's a battleground that one needs to be victorious over every day. Victory is always sweet, but defeat is just a part of life. I have had triumphs and failures which I won't be able to pen down in this prologue, as I could quite literally write an entire book out of it, but I would definitely give a timeline. In 2018, when I was 10 years old, but my mind, well, not so young, went through one of the most gut-wrenching things in life, and that's when I started writing in bits and pieces. I didn't write long stories or poetry, but just quotes here and there.

Whenever I had a nightmare or anything, I would journal my thoughts and pen down my feelings. It sort of became a coping mechanism and helped me take a grip on my brimming emotions, and helped me see things clearly. I did that for a while, not every day, but whenever I was feeling overwhelmed. In 2021, I developed a flair for reading and expanding my horizons. There was this thing for burning the midnight oil in me, and I constantly wanted to learn and learn. Any hardship does not leave without a lesson. In 2021, I was a reformed person, and the wisdom in me was visible through every word I used to speak then. I was healed from what I went through. This continued for a while with droplets of rain, but the sun never set regardless. In 2023, I went through a traumatic experience, which was different, but the post-traumatic feeling would always hit me in instances; however, it helped me master the art of detachment. But you don't become wise in the click of a finger, it made me take a step back in every aspect and deformed me completely. I turned into a different person and constantly hated myself. In the beginning, I didn't get anything out of it, but slowly and gradually, I stopped caring so much so that I was afraid of my very own self. This paved the way for me to write poetry and dive even more into my philosophical side.

I thought and thought, so much that I could see through things at a deeper level, whether it's the world, myself or my emotions. Whenever I would write poetry, it would always feel like my thoughts had been given shape, and I would instantly feel relieved, and it would provide me with clarity. At first, I would only write about my emotions and feelings, but eventually, I would also write about the world from a third-person perspective. It would also make me realise how big the world is and how small I am as an individual. How internally we are so deep, and how everything has a reason at the same. I am still not as wise as I aspire to be, I am still not completely reformed or healed, but I am still me, and I shall continue to learn and unlearn no matter what.

Most of the poems that you will read might seem pessimistic at first glance, but wisdom is never brought through happy tears, being robust comes from losing in the battleground as we prepare for the next fight with caution.

If you are suffering through anything, try jotting down your thoughts or finding a coping mechanism because escape is never the solution; it provides us with cheap dopamine and puts us into a deep end where everything seems dark, and one can cry for help but not help themselves. This book is a compilation of poetry and many issues, whether it's being insecure, love, war, melancholy, etc, are mentioned. It's a short read, but I hope it will be introspective for you.

A massive hourglass

The sand is returning to its origin

Slowly and gradually

Life is repeating its cycle

Of pleasure and misery;

Turn the hourglass upside down

Which side will bring me

All for what I greed?

Two perspectives, similar shape

Both identical,

Yet such a hard choice to make.

Behind all misery,

Behind all pain,

I believe, there exists a world,

Which can free me from disdain.

Behind all the tears

Behind all the desolations

I believe, there exists a world

Where happiness prevails.

If I could go to one place

Drive all the sorrows away

I would sprint and sprint,

And move from thy world,

Far far away.

When the world is against a task,

When they say

If you do this

Your life will fall apart;

Yet we let the rebellious soul out

Challenge the shatter

Let it burn your world down

They said, Beware;

But I am the master and the player.

Behind that smile,

The pain she hides,

The melancholy of a broken heart,

The symphony of a silent melody.

They told me I'd never make it,
That I was destined to fail.
They whispered, "You're nothing."
But I still stood tall.
My hands trembled as they held the ink,
Painting my future across a blank wall,
While their voices roared in the distance,
And I rose higher than them all.

The tremors of fear,

When heartache seized the day,

When hands shook

And stole my slumber away

I took out my notebook

And opened a new world

For me to stay.

One day, we see the sun

One day, the pain burns

One day, the anxiety goes into flames

One day, the tremor leaves the place

The shallowness of a broken heart

The words which the mouth

can't seem to start

The speechlessness in the long monologues

The silence is so, so loud.

When you lose consciousness

You allow the world to do as it pleases

When the surroundings try to disfigure you,

You accept their words with utter defeat.

Even when you lose your mind,

Don't let your heart seek,

What wasn't meant for it from the very beginning.

I remember the night
I dug my nails in my hand,
From fear and self-doubt
I could hardly withstand.
From agitation, embarrassment,
And the taste of defeat
Each trembling breath
Felt too heavy, too deep.
Those marks healed by morning,
But my heart kept its song
Still racing, still aching,
For far, far too long.

Even if I survive

Then what am I to live for

Even when I laugh

Why am I not happy

The soul feels lost

Wanting to be found

So much silence

Yet so loud

Where are my daffodils

Where is my serendipity

Why am I with so many

Yet so alone.

What is life?

Life is infinite

To love and beyond

Even when we don't believe in it

But if we don't seize to believe in love

Then what's life made for

Live up to all the pleasures

Seek what life has to offer

Its endless

Its to infinity and beyond

Go live up

To reap it

You're made for all that

You're the symphony

Of the soft caressing

Of them tulip fields.

Is this the way through life?

Sleeping it off.

Replacing the awakened nightmares

With dreams of sunflower fields

Colouring my way through life

Finding comfort in discomfort

Energizing through lethargy

Chortling through pain

The deep end has beckoned me

To find slumber in its arms

Yet the solace is nowhere to be found

When will the colourful fields

Bring lustre to thy colourless life?

Love is beauty

Which some adore from far sight

And some experience it very fine

Some witness the comforts of it

Some experience the pain

So deep it is and yet so shallow

So bright it is and yet so dull

It goes away in a twinkle of a star

And allures your way in a heartbeat

From Oh so far!

It prevails yet departs

So much pleasure

But still haunts the ways of the heart.

Reaping the comforts of delusions

Forgetting about the path

The soul is numb and so is mind

The heart is void and so is life

Is this the only way to find solace

Of heart, mind and body?

The waves of the heart

Struggle to find layers in the brain,

Of passion and peace

But rummaging through it

Only one thing can be seen

Oh so vivid

Oh so white

So much pain, yet so much pride.

The teardrop fell

I reached out for a wipe

It fell again

And it reached my shirt

When I thought I could control it

Someone saw

I made my way out of there

To find a spot

I wanted to cry

Yet I failed to find a bolthole

I walked away

While rain started to pour on its way

My heart felt relieved

I cried all the sorrow away

I walked and walked and walked

Till solace seized the day.

The poor doze their lives off

To imagine what life is

Close to all the luxuries

The ones who own the comforts

Doze their days off

To imagine what life is

In tranquillity and peace

We all escape to a world

Oh so immaculate–

Daydreaming of all the awakened wish fulfilments

Once the eye opens, the bloomed floors evade,

And autumn seizes the day

The sprinting trees, turn into seedlings

And the fishes which once swam in the vast expanse of salty waters

Suffocate in their little jars.

Envisaging the best

Seeking no help

Wondering if I'll make it

All by myself

Will I win this battle?

And achieve all I want?

Will the stars align in my favour

Or catch me off guard?

Why do we run up to someone?

When we win

Why do we seek validation?

When we lose

Why do we do as they say?

Why do we live up to conventions?

Why do we please people so much?

Why do we seek so much from externalities?

When we are alone

When we are ourselves

The truth is let out

The soul yearns to dance,

The heart wishes to rush,

The mind wishes to play,

And the stars want to shine,

Bright as a diamond,

Soulful as a melody,

The joy enters

And the anguish escapes.

Vanish with a few words

The betrayal and dismay

Sink like a ship under ocean waves

The envy and hatred,

The animosity and evilness

Are lost when fake apologies come our way

Don't let the lover fool you

For you are too vulnerable

To be left astray.

Your well-wishers don't hurt you

For those who do

They are sent by the universe as lessons

Which we never learn.

Holding my emotions within,

Thought emotion is for the frail,

I held on for a towering time,

but had to let go one day.

Constantly doubting oneself,

Being unaware of my worth,

When I see my reflection in the mirror,

The insecurity sabotages the one.

I held on as long as I could,

Despising every part of me,

Undermining my capabilities,

Living in denial of what a true self I could be.

Today I let go,

Accepted the one in the view,

Realized how it's meant to shine,

And radiates like the moon.

I gravitate towards a positive life,

Will made of iron

And born to shine.

My life will flourish like gold mines

No one can stop me,

Not even life.

Playing dress up in my room,

Me all dolled up,

Music to my ears,

Am I the prettiest girl?

Trying to be a song lyric,

Wanting to look like a dream,

Oh to be a seeker of beauty,

Is so so heavenly.

Why is the heart so used to its surroundings?

It will even choose a vicinity familiar,

Above the one with a bed of roses.

It is used to the pain,

which it can not let go of,

for what is meant to save its day.

It holds on to the worse

Preventing it from seeing the sun.

When I lie in my bed,

Everything feels like a catastrophic end.

The four walls of my room,

Confine me, in my suffocating head.

No one knows when I will escape this cycle,

Yet the optimism doesn't seem to end.

The world has a different dimension,

When I am losing in every sense.

Failed in many aspects,

Yet the pride doesn't seem to come to an end.

Yesternight, I wore a satin robe to bed
When I placed myself on white silk sheets,
I felt a tender caress,
The slumber felt serene,
But my dreams left me in distress,
I woke up in ambiguity,
From that wild, wild mishap
How ironic it is
My peaceful slumber was ruined,
Yet my body felt like a thunderstorm wrapped in grace
Touched my soul with no name, no hands, no face
But it pierced through my soul like a devil's gaze
It left a scent of musk embrace,
And my heart felt a sudden change.

I was sipping my dawn's zeal,

When I heard a breaking sound.

It slipped away from my hands,

Like a thunder cloud.

The somnolence was taken aback,

The body was jittery,

The tumbler was in shreds,

And so were the associated memories.

I stood at the top, wanting more than the view,
So I pushed myself hard, like all legends do.
Chased the goals with my heart open wide,
Believing the stars would fall into my stride.
But despair answered when I reached out to fate,
And the skies, once mine, just watched me break.
My wings gave up, and down I fell;
From fire to fog, to a quiet kind of hell.
I folded my hands, whispered to the skies,
Asking for strength, for the will to rise.
Ambiguity wrapped me tight, hope dimmed its light,
And the girl who once glowed was fading from sight.
They took what I had my shine, my sway,
But not who I was... that never fades away.
Because deep in the mess, the ache, the grey;
I was always enough to find my own way.

I take a step forward

A leash binds me

Controls me like a puppet,

Puts me behind.

I take a step forward

Someone traps me,

I fall again,

And getting up seems unattained.

The beauty of stars,

The comfort of gazing,

The definition of the blurred view,

The fantasy of night,

Left untold since ages.

The wind the breeze blowing through the hair,

Makes one fly away,

In the depth of darkness.

The smell of success,

The oath to win,

The dopamine on receiving the prize,

The heart race of competing,

To sprit of winning;

Oh my days

I would give it all to be a part of this rat-race.

So simple is the world,

Yet we complicate it so much.

The duplicity of the illusions

Feed our way through dearth.

The northern lights,

The Antarctic life,

Expanse of landscapes,

Gigantic sights–

Stay undiscovered

In the shallowness since birth.

The aurora effect of the sky

The enchanting visible sights.

The ethereality of nature–

The power to heal,

The strength to destroy.

Lies undiscovered,

When one gives up on such profound joy,

The cluttered brain

Never gets to see

Such lovely days.

Giving up all to see the bright sun

In this finite life.

We forget

in the darkness of the night

The stars twinkle, infinite.

The giganticity of the waves

Fail to disrupt the comforted slumber of the human race.

The scenic beauty is underestimated

In the vast city landscapes.

Your words echo,

In the whispers of the mountains

On the roads, oh! so treacherous

They are a reminder

Of a little solace-filled embrace

The comforting sounds of your voice

Still drive the high tides away

The laughter caused by you

Still wrenches the heart

Ever since you've left

The world didn't really fall apart

The memories hold the power

To help the grey heart

They fill the room with tadow

Whenever your name is asked

So much distance there is

Yet the fire ignites wherever you are.

The little girl walked in orphan shoes,

She saw a boy with no Monday blues,

She had a change of heart,

When she saw two grown-ups holding his arm.

He screamed at them, and she whispered loudly

Oh, to have caretakers makes it such a happy town.

She wore gold bangles when the bomb fell
Now they glint in some ghost town shell
A child's shoe lies by a shattered wall
Just souvenirs from a nation's fall

The air smells burnt. Not fire, but skin
Hearts carved hollow, bones worn thin
One prayed, one ran, one froze
Now each one sleeps in dust and clothes

No funeral march, no names on stone
Only ash that screams in undertone
A thousand lives for one regime
Don't dress it up, war isn't a dream

A drone above, a mother below
She kissed her son, then let him go
Now,
Silence sings a lullaby
And I write what the world lets die.

A house is not a home
when the couch runs empty,
its cushions carrying only
the ghost of a touch,
The silence is louder than any voice.

The eyes whisper melancholy
not in words,
but in glances that flicker
through the smoke of memory,
chortling through laughter long extinguished.

The mattress remembers.
It once roared with joy,
with bodies tangled in careless dawns,
with shrieks of laughter
that cracked open the sky.

But now
it creaks beneath the weight of absence,
soaking in the dusk
where pain drips slow,
a steady rain no one listens to.

A house is not a home.

It is brick and wood,

a hollow ribcage without a beating heart.

Home lives only

in the echo of love

that no longer lingers here.

Envious I've been of the ones around me,
Why be surrounded by light when darkness has found me?
What have I not done that they have to see,
the colour that fades and stays black within me?

What have I not prayed that they prayed with might,
to see wishes granted while I lose the fight?
I suffer my hell, a silence I keep,
while envy turns hearts into shadows that weep.

Envy makes you evil, but I will not fall,
my moral ground stands, I still wish them all.
While they sing my downfall's lullaby, sly,
I rise in the venom, unbroken, I try

Beauty is incomparable,
it deceives the way of hearts.
It lures you in within seconds,
then watches you fall apart.

It turns soft hearts into ashes,
and sweetness into poison.
It glows from afar, makes you yearn,
while it dims your inner horizon.

It's something you crave for yourself,
yet it steals what's within you whole.
For beauty may dazzle the crowd,
but it quietly robs your soul.

Don't fear losing what was never yours, we come
empty-handed,
and we leave the same,
our graves gilded in gold,
yet hollow, no shame.

Don't seek to cure your dismay
in material illusions;
the soul leaves only
its mark of memories.

For all the fleeting pleasures,
the illusions,
the temporary shine, what remains eternal
is never what we own,
but what we leave behind.

They say life changes you, yes, it does,
and makes you reach heights, etches, and burns
because.
Once you experience the taste of both sides,
you fail to see where your true soul resides.

Does it glow in the beauty and warmth of the day,
or in the night where shadows hold sway?
The person remains, not faltering from sight,
enduring the dark, embracing the light.

The weather may shiver, a frantic ride,
but while I am breathing, with nowhere to hide
the storm that I carry, no matter the tide,
will never desert me, it stays by my side.

Message from the Author

Closing Note

Hey there,

If you've reached this page, I want to take a moment to thank you from the very core of my heart for walking with me through this journey. By now, I'm sure you already have a fair introduction of who I am, not just from my prologue but through every poem, every line, and every fragment that spilled out of me onto these pages. Poetry, for me, has always been more than words it is memory stitched with emotion, it is silence made visible, it is truth that dares to exist without disguise.

I believe every book is a conversation between the writer and the reader. I've spoken in metaphors, in broken truths, in confessions hidden between the lines but a conversation works both ways. I cannot hear your thoughts directly, but I long to know how my words touched you, challenged you, or maybe even unsettled you. That is why I humbly request you to leave a review on Amazon, BlueRose.com, or Flipkart. Not for numbers, not for vanity, but so I can see the reflection of my work in your eyes. So I can learn what resonated, what wisdom reached you, and what parts of myself I still need to unlearn.

This journey has been long, and at times, heavy. I poured myself into these poems so much that I often lost track of where the words ended and where I began. There were nights when the lines became mirrors, and I found myself staring back at me through my own writing, sometimes a stranger, sometimes a friend. That, I believe, is the true beauty of nonfiction poetry. It doesn't fabricate; it reveals. It doesn't invent; it remembers. And in that remembering, it teaches us who we really are.

I hope while reading these pages you found pieces of yourself too. Maybe in a metaphor that clung to you. Maybe in a single line that felt like it was written only for you. If that happens, then my purpose is fulfilled.

If there's one truth I want to leave you with, it's this: what we think, we become. Turbulence will come. Storms will rage. Darkness will visit. But within you lies the power to create light, again and again. This is not blind optimism, it's lived experience. Every page I've written carries scars, questions, and prayers but also resilience. So, as we part here, I hope you find your happiness and hold onto it fiercely. I hope you leave behind the burdens that were never yours to carry. And I hope, above all, you never stop searching for yourself in words, in memories, in love, in silence. Because the truest journey is the one that always leads us back home to ourselves.

Thank you for walking with me. This is not the end it is only a pause, until our words meet again.

With love and honesty,
Naunidh Sachdeva